HOW TO WRITE A SIZZLING SYNOPSIS

BRYAN COHEN

This publication is protected under the US Copyright Act of 1976 and all other applicable international, federal, state and local laws, and all rights are reserved, including resale rights: you are not allowed to give or sell this book to anyone else. If you received this publication from anyone other than Bryan Cohen, Amazon or Best Page Forward , you've received a pirated copy. Please contact us via the website and notify us of the situation.

All contents Copyright © 2016 by Bryan Cohen and Best Page Forward LLC. All rights reserved. No part of this document or the related files may be reproduced or transmitted in any form, by any means (electronic, photocopying, recording, or otherwise) without the prior written permission of the publisher.

Limit of Liability and Disclaimer of Warranty: The publisher has used its best efforts in preparing this book, and the information provided herein is provided "as is." Bryan Cohen and Build Creative Writing Ideas make no representation or warranties with respect to the accuracy or completeness of the contents of this book and specifically disclaims any implied warranties of merchantability or fitness for any particular purpose and shall in no event be liable for any loss of profit or any other commercial damage, including but not limited to special, incidental, consequential, or other damages. All characters appearing in this work are fictitious. Any resemblance to real persons, living or dead, is purely coincidental.

Trademarks: This book identifies product names and services known to be trademarks, registered trademarks, or service marks of their respective holders. They are used throughout this book in an editorial fashion only. In addition, terms suspected of being trademarks, registered trademarks, or service marks have been appropriately capitalized, although Bryan Cohen and Build Creative Writing Ideas cannot attest to the accuracy of this information. Use of a term in this book should not be regarded as affecting the validity of any trademark, registered trademark, or service mark. Bryan Cohen and Build Creative Writing Ideas are not associated with any product or vendor mentioned in this book.

Finally, use your head. Nothing in this book is intended to replace common sense, legal, medical or other professional advice, and is meant to inform and entertain the reader. So have fun with the book and happy writing!

Copyright © 2016 Bryan Cohen

All rights reserved.

ISBN: 1540345408

ISBN-13: 978-1540345400

Table of Contents

Introduction	5
The Synopsis Mindset	13
What's the Point of the Synopsis?	19
How Do I Simplify My Plot?	27
What's Important Enough to Include?	35
How Do I Make It Sound Good?	47
How Do I Make My Synopsis Grow From Beginning to End?	57
How Do I End Things with a Bang?	65
What's a Step-by-Step System I Can Use for My Synopsis?	75
How Do I Edit My Synopsis Down to the Essential?	81
How Long Should My Synopsis Be, Where Should I Use It, and Other Common Considerations	89
What Else Goes Into the Description?	97
Appendix: Additional Synopsis Examples	103
About the Author	115
Acknowledgements	117
Thanks From Bryan	119

Introduction

Have you ever wondered how a reader chooses to buy a certain book? Well, it's actually a pretty simple process. First, the reader takes a look at the cover. If the cover is exceptional, then the customer will look at the book reviews. Usually, if you have enough reviews and a high enough star rating, then the reader will dive into the selling tool you have the most control over. This is the exact moment your potential reader takes a look at your description.

Don't get me wrong, covers are incredible for getting attention. When you're trying to make headway in a new genre, making sure that your cover looks as good as, if not better than, the other covers in there, is extremely important. And when you have a high number of reviews, you keep the reader stuck to the page, as if he's saying, "Looks good. What else you got?"

But it's the synopsis that sells your book.

Mark Dawson, who is a bajillion-copy-selling thriller author, once surveyed over 10,000 of his readers to find out how they became his fans. His results were a little bit surprising. His survey asked readers whether they came in from looking at his covers, checking out his reviews, reading his descriptions, and so on.

What he found was that close to five times as many readers bought his books because of his descriptions as did the fans who snatched them because of the covers. Five times as many people read the description and said, "This guy's for me." We tend to stress a lot about covers, and maybe even more about reviews, but we might be looking in the wrong place. When a reader is choosing between two books with the same number of reviews and the same general quality of book cover, it's actually the book description that makes the difference.

From personal experience, I can say that focusing on book descriptions changed my career in amazing, unforeseen ways.

Let me introduce myself. I'm Bryan Cohen and I get around. I started self-publishing back in the unwieldy toddler phase of the indie movement (circa 2010). I started out by publishing a series of nonfiction books filled with ideas to beat writer's block. In mid-2014, I began co-hosting the *Sell More Books Show* with Councilman Jim "Shawty" Kukral. With over 100 episodes under our belts, we've learned an incredible amount about the news of self-publishing, and countless tips from around the industry. We've also built up a dedicated base of fans (hey, fans!). After starting the show, I went on to write five novels using the tips I picked up every single week, which allowed me to dance around several bestseller lists and accumulate over 400,000 downloads for the books across my catalog.

But none of that really matters here.

What's important about my specs is that starting around 2009, I began a productive career in copywriting. I wrote thousands of articles for a variety of blogs before I really hit my sweet spot as a ghostwriter for publications like Entrepreneur, Forbes, Inc., and Mashable. It was during these years that I put in a good chunk of my Malcolm Gladwell-esque 10,000 hours of copywriting expertise.

In mid-2015, Rocking Self Publishing co-host Simon Whistler advised me to take my copywriting to the next level. He said, "Hey man, why are you doing this copywriting stuff when your true passion is helping authors? You should do copywriting for authors." Simon Whistler is a smart guy.

During the next calendar year, I wrote over 300 book descriptions for other authors. It's been a wild ride across every possible genre, from "active" Western romance to spiritual nonfiction books. By spending all of this time copywriting for other authors, I've really learned where most writers struggle in this business. When it comes down to it, they hate writing blurbs*.

> * For the purposes of this book, I'll use the terms blurb, description, and product summary interchangeably. Purists may point out that some of these terms are incorrect, but when it comes down to it, authors just use all these terms in a jumble anyway. Words are hard sometimes!

There are three main reasons authors have trouble crafting a compelling description for their books.

They are as follows:

1. Authors absolutely hate writing them.

For some reason, the whole process feels completely wrong. They've been spending so much time thinking about their word count and their deadlines that they can't even fathom why it would take 10 hours to churn out a 200-word description. Therefore, they hate it.

2. The description they write is too long, wordy, and rambling.

What most authors don't realize is that when a synopsis meanders, readers assume the book is a wandering mess. And when the book description is confusing, they assume the plot of the book is confusing as well.

3. They write descriptions that are all about the plot, and nothing but the plot.

Unless you're writing about an expertly crafted whodunit, it's very rare to hear the biggest fans of a novel rave about the plot. You're much more likely to hear about the emotions readers felt, and the characters they identified with. When authors focus too much on the plot, readers may imagine that the book is missing the things they enjoy so much about the novels they love: identifiable characters and emotional connection.

If you've ever checked out any of my videos or handouts on book descriptions, you know that I like to use a four-part system for my descriptions. The synopsis is one part of that system. But I'm not here to tell you that my way is the best or the only method for writing these product summaries. Since the synopsis is issue #1 for most writers, this book is solely dedicated to getting the synopsis right.

It's very possible that you might throw a bit of a hissy fit because you have to read an entire book about writing a 200-word summary for your novel or novella. You might be saying, "How much can there be to say? You just write the damn thing and then people buy your book." Well, if it was that easy, then we'd all be doing it. Trust me when I say I've seen a very large sample size of book descriptions in both traditional and self-publishing. From that anecdotal research, I've determined that most book descriptions suck. One of my purposes in life is to teach authors better ways of doing things so they stop sucking… I mean, "causing themselves hardships on the marketing side of things."

Summarizing your book in such a way that it sells more copies isn't complicated science or some art form that only geniuses possess. Writing a synopsis is part of a system that has rules, and following those rules can lead to better results.

I hope that this book opens your eyes to what's possible when you write a better synopsis that actually makes your book sound good (roll credits). Thank you so much for picking up this book. Please enjoy it responsibly.

Sincerely,

Bryan

HOW TO WRITE A SIZZLING SYNOPSIS

BRYAN COHEN

The Synopsis Mindset

Without fail, whenever I poke around on the Internet looking for information on writing book descriptions, there is a certain meme I find myself always coming across. In this viral sensation, there's a captioned picture of Gollum from Lord of the Rings. The caption on the picture reads as follows: "We know we must writes the blurb, but we hates it!"

So why do we all feel like Gollum? For the less fantasy-minded among us, here's another way to phrase that question: "Why is writing the description so freakin' hard?"

After all, when you've been plugging away on your first (or 50th) novel, you've probably gotten into a rhythm at some point where it seems easier. Some people will call this "the flow state." I know from experience that the flow state is a beautiful phenomenon that allows you to write twice as fast and with significantly better characterization, setting, and witty one-liners. When you sit down to write a blurb, it feels like all that flow is gone. Except for the flow of expletives from your mouth when your description sounds terrible.

What you need to understand is that writing your blurb is a form of copywriting. And for the brain of most authors, copywriting is about as foreign a writing style as Latin is to today's elementary school students (won't somebody think of the children?). Your brain loves the familiar. If it had its choice, it would rather do the same thing all of the time. When you've been writing for years on end, even if it isn't easy, it's certainly easier now than when you just started out. If you've only written blurbs for 10 books or fewer, then you've essentially just started. And that's going to make your brain very unhappy.

If you're truly interested in writing better book descriptions on your own, then you absolutely must go into the description-writing process as if it's something new that you're willing to learn. If you're angry that it doesn't come easily, then you're going to have as much success as the whiny kid in class who forgot to study his Latin conjugations. Carpe Diem, everybody! You've got to do the work before you can reap the benefits.

So, why doesn't a synopsis feel like the same kind of writing as your novel or novella? For one, you're not describing a story. There's no dialogue, and the only character is the "narrator" of the description. That brings us to the second point, which is that you're not speaking as the author of this book. You're acting more like an employee for your publishing company who has to say good things about someone else's work. For the modest among us, we're about as interested in praising ourselves as we are prancing down a winter street completely naked.

Thirdly, blurbs are not always A to B all the way to Z when it comes to your plot. For a synopsis to have the highest possible impact, you need to pick and choose what plot to include. Sometimes, you need to skip major plot points just to make sure you don't say too much. In many cases, this means leaving out important characters or speaking in a general way about very specific world building terms (i.e., place names, religions, five-part character names, etc.). If you deep dive too far into the specifics of your story, you may scare away readers for fear of the book being too dense and incomprehensible.

Let's jump into a little Stuart Smalley self-help here (stay with me, it's not a very long book). Writing the blurb isn't hard because you're stupid or because you're a bad writer. I know you aren't stupid because you bought this book (duh). It's also very likely that you aren't terrible. And if you are, good news... you can get much, much better over time!

If you aren't stupid, and you're probably not a poor writer, then why is the blurb so difficult?

Two reasons. The first is that you can't write a blurb because it's unfamiliar to your brain. And the second is that you have yet to learn the guidelines for writing the most effective synopsis. When you follow the steps in this book, you'll learn the rules and you'll start to get the experience you need to get more readers on board. This book includes examples you can learn from in multiple genres. We've got exercises at the end of each chapter that will further reinforce the points you should take home. I'm doing everything I can in this book to save you having to go through 10,000 hours like I have with my copywriting. You can absolutely make a great deal of progress in a short period of time. But I recommend you take action, and that starts with the first exercise here in Chapter 1.

I know, you're itching to get to the next chapter to dive into the good stuff. But I really wish I could guilt you into doing all of the exercises. Skipping the exercises in a book is like going to dance classes and just leering at people from the corner. It's creepy and a waste of your money.

Here's the first one. I swear it'll take a few minutes at most:

Exercise #1: Find the oldest piece of your writing you have access to (scour that hard drive). Give it a read. I realize that this may be painful. Compare that piece of

How to Write a Sizzling Synopsis

writing to the latest writing you've completed. Assign a percentage to how much you've improved. As you start writing your blurbs, remember that you can improve by at least that percentage if you put your time and energy into getting better at copywriting.

Recap:
- Writing your synopsis is hard because your brain has yet to be trained in copywriting.
- Be willing to learn and do the exercises in the book to make improvements.
- Bryan is guilting you from afar to do all the exercises.

What's the Point of the Synopsis?

Let's say a friend of yours has read a book or watched a movie that you've never heard of. A normal person might then ask that friend what the movie is about. Which of the following three responses do you expect to hear:

1. A point-by-point summary that takes 5 to 10 minutes to deliver?
2. A comprehensive list of the names, places, and themes this piece of art contains?
3. Or just the bullet points?

Life is far too short to choose anything other than number three, and yet, we tend to choose differently when we create a synopsis for our own books. Why should we expect to deliver anything different than what normal people expect in real life? A synopsis is meant to convey these bullet points in an entertaining and emotional way. That's it. I could stop there and end the chapter, but I want to give you a little more information. It's just the kind of guy I am.

Connect with Readers

You don't have to lie to me. You want to be as successful as JK Rowling or Stephen King. We didn't go into this to be a mid-lister or a bottom lister... or a bottom feeder. But we need to keep things in perspective here. For most of us, we're not going to be able to reach every person in the world the way Harry Potter or The Hunger Games has. It's significantly more effective to target the voracious readers who always have a hardcover or an e-reader in their hands. Fortunately for us, each genre has voracious readers who really identify with the characters and themes in that particular genre. In order to reach them, we must provide some kind of emotional experience that connects with those readers.

When you write a synopsis, you want the characters to be relatable. That doesn't mean they have to be friendly and funny. Just look at Don Draper (the subject of at least 20,000 memes on Facebook). What it means is that we want readers to recognize that character as someone from their lives, identify a variation of a character they've read before, or we want them to want to be that character. Think about it. Readers are often reading to either process their lives or find some form of escape. They want to know the hero or they want to be the hero.

Let's take a look at an example that illustrates this point:

> **Bad Example:** Katniss Everdeen lives in District 12, one of the 12 districts controlled by the Capitol.
>
> **Good Example:** Katniss Everdeen is a survivor.

Now the prose-writing author in you may really want to use example #1 as the first line in your synopsis. This is an instinct you should suppress when writing blurbs. The problem with the first example is that we've found out nothing with an emotional resonance about our main character. Since about 80% of people on the Internet stop reading things after the first line, we better make a stronger impact right off the bat.

Example #2, however, allows us to identify with our protagonist. We don't need to know all of the specifics about her drab home or the death of her father. We just need to give the reader something identifiable to go on. While calling someone a survivor is a little vague, it brings with it all sorts of emotional connections for readers in all walks of life. In the acting world, we would call this substitution. In writing a synopsis, I would call it the right thing to do.

Feeling Connected

Even if you haven't experienced this much yourself, voracious readers can have an itchy "buying finger." Particularly in the romance genre, readers who eat pages for breakfast will read many, many books. Just look at the downfall of subscription reading service Scribd for a real-world example of this. The service literally had to stop doing a subscription model because romance readers were putting them out of business. For voracious readers of all genres, however, these powerful purchasers still need some reason to make that purchase. When you provide them with a character they can relate to, it makes the reader feel more comfortable. This way, the reader knows the book isn't too far off base from what they've read before.

I realize that what I just said may not sound particularly artistic, but there've been plenty of studies conducted on just this point. In Charles Duhigg's book The Power of Habit, he discussed how when people listen to music, their brain actually craves the familiar. Songs that are too unfamiliar, like the ones that combine new genres together to create something unique, make listeners change the radio dial. No matter how much they might enjoy "Hey Ya," they'll stick with "My Heart Will Go On" because that's what their brains are used to ("Never let go, brain. Never let go."). As much as we want to say we'll read the most unique stuff in the world, because we're so darn cultural, we're actually creatures of habit down to the molecular level.

What does all this mean? It means that if your book sounds too unique, it may actually hurt you! This may not matter much if you have 10,000+ readers on your mailing list, but if you're just starting out, this is not the time to celebrate how many genre lines your book crosses. It's time to fulfill what the people want.

It's important to note that it's okay if your book isn't for everybody. You may wonder how many potential readers you could lose if your book conforms strictly to one genre or a certain type of fiction. It's true. You will lose readers, and thank goodness for that. You don't want everyone to read your book. I repeat, you do not want everyone to read your book, because if you write Western romance and a sci-fi reader checks it out, you'll probably get one of those one-star reviews that says, "This book is not for me." It's in your best interest to collect the readers who will like your book the most. We can worry about taking over the world with a mega-bestseller later on.

Paperback Versus Online

One last point I want to make is where you should physically put a synopsis. One of the top questions I get from authors is whether or not they need a separate description on their back cover and their online sales page. Personally, I think this is a question that is becoming irrelevant in the digital age.

I'm not sure why a back cover synopsis and an online synopsis ever needed to be different. You're trying to accomplish the same thing in both, so why give yourself extra work? Secondly, you're so unlikely to sell copies of your book based off a unique back cover description (unless somebody finds it in the remains of a hollowed-out 2017 Barnes & Noble), that it's never going to matter, so you shouldn't worry about it at all.

Put your synopsis wherever you need a synopsis. There's no need for multiple versions. A synopsis is meant to tell readers what they should expect, much like you would tell a friend the bullet points of a movie. If that friend says, "Wow, that sounds good," then you've done your job as a synopsis writer.

Let's do the scariest thing we can think of. Let's write a synopsis now, before I've given you any pointers on doing it right.

> **Exercise #2:** Write a basic summary of the book you are most interested in selling right now. Do as little thinking as possible during the process. It's imperative that you do this exercise before moving on, because we're going to use it in many of our later exercises.

Recap:

- A synopsis is less of a point-by-point summary and more like a series of bullet points.
- Conveying identifiable characters in your synopsis will appeal to the voracious readers in your genre.
- Don't worry about being unique, because most people read what's familiar to them.
- It's ok to write something that isn't "for everyone."
- Start with just one version of your synopsis. Don't think about writing a second version for your back cover, because they can be the same.

How Do I Simplify My Plot?

Imagine that you've finally scored that dream meeting with a big-time movie producer. Like most pitch clichés, this one takes place in an elevator. You know your story forward and backward, and you can't wait to tell him everything there is to know about your book. I may not know many movie producers myself, but I do know if you actually were to tell him everything, this producer would be doing everything in his power to get out of that elevator, possibly even plummeting to his death to avoid hearing about one more side character or one more subplot.

Does that mean I'm saying you should avoid writing complicated stories in the first place? No, not at all. Complex characters and plots are awesome, but you don't need to include all of them in a simple sellable synopsis.

Complicated romances, thrillers, mysteries, and horror novels have it relatively easy. Even in the most complex of these stories, you generally have a basic framework for a certain plot. Romance involves a guy and girl getting together, thrillers include some bad guy doing something terrible and an awesome hero saving the day. Mysteries usually contain crime, followed by someone figuring out the solution. Horror shows a bad guy or gal killing people and the protagonists trying to escape, etc. etc. Authors who write in these genres can keep to this framework and end up with a pretty succinct synopsis.

It's when you start getting into the complex worlds of sci-fi and fantasy that authors tend to run into trouble. These books often have so many characters and subplots they would make Shakespeare roll over in his fancy British grave. I have nothing against these books. I've read James Michener... and enjoyed it! What you need to keep in mind is that no matter how important you think they are, you do not need to have every character and every location referenced in your synopsis. In most cases, you can simply follow the main two or three characters. And if it's an ensemble piece... the same thing holds true. No more than two or three characters. Anything more than two or three is way too many.

In the next chapter, I'll go into the nitty-gritty of how to narrow down what is important and what isn't, but in the meantime let me give you some general rules of what needs to go in the essential version of your story.

Please do not break these rules unless you've sold more than 100,000 books. No cheating for you 90k sellers out there!

Only Explain Character Details That Are Relevant

It would not be completely out of the question to present some synopses as character résumés. I've seen characters with so many qualifications noted in the first few sentences that I'd be more than willing to hire them for a job. The problem is, I would never read that book. You need to get into the meaty details in your synopsis almost right away, and spending too much time elaborating on your character's every virtue wastes time and space. I've even taken to the idea to mentioning my characters by just their first name (no last name or middle name) and trait for that character before I move on to the good stuff. You don't have to go that far, but you do have to know when enough is enough.

Avoid Using Names and Places That Don't Matter to the Full Story

You know that old memory experiment where scientists try to see how many playing cards average people can remember before they start to forget the first one? The gist of it is, we can only keep two or three main things running in our heads at any given time. It makes me think of that Married with Children episode where Christina Applegate's Kelly Bundy couldn't learn a new fact without removing one of the old facts. Readers are kind of like Kelly in this way. If you introduce too many names and places in your synopsis, it's going to be very hard for them to keep track of everything.

I've seen a lot of synopses that will mention a character's name who isn't even relevant to the plot. This can take the form of an ex-girlfriend who broke up with the character in the first page never to be heard from again or a third-level thug who is easily dispatched by the third chapter. You have a choice: fill your reader's head with increasing emotional momentum and excitement OR the names of five main characters in your fantasy novel. I hope by now you know which one to choose. If mentioning a character will not enrich your potential fan's synopsis-reading experience, then you should save it for the book. In fact, that's a great mantra to highlight here:

> When in doubt, save it for the book.

Avoid Highlighting Subplots That Don't Warrant the Attention

I see a pretty common problem arise when authors try to incorporate what they believe is an important subplot in their synopses. They introduce this "pit stop" that takes the heroes away from their main objective, which forces them to take several sentences to introduce place names and side characters that don't matter. Well, this little pit stop is the same exact place where prospective readers click away.

It's much better to spend your time focusing more on the development of the protagonist and how his or her emotions tie into the main plot. Leave the side characters' subplots in the book.

If you absolutely must mention a location or character to give your synopsis the necessary context, consider avoiding having to put another fact into your reader's head. Instead of naming a villain or a character, refer to them by their title or as an enemy or friend.

* * *

A Magical Option for Fantasy Writers

Here's one last point about fantasy. What can I say? You guys and gals write some long freaking books, which makes your efforts to cut down a synopsis a bit more difficult. Here is a last-ditch effort if you can't possibly cut down your synopsis to 2-3 main characters and one main plot. Leave them all out.

To keep the complications out of your description about the world, simply use general mythological terms. I've seen series starters of big-time fantasy epics like The Wheel of Time and Game of Thrones use this exact method to great effect. They simply have too many characters and points of views to make a description make sense. So all they talk about is the world and what's going on in the vaguest of vague terms.

Here's an example:

> The Age of Elf has ended after countless millennia, leaving man to rule with iron and fire. War is constant and blood is spilled in every village across the land. But some magic remains in the untouched realm. It rises unseen in the East, and it may become too powerful for a divided mankind to face. What the world needs is a hero to unite them all...

These are not my favorite kinds of descriptions, but at least they're simple and easy to identify with. Consider this your tempting red-button option to use if you can't possibly chop down what you have in store for your readers.

Remember that when push comes to shove, your job is not to explain the book. You should leave that to the book reviewers. Your only job with a synopsis is to get readers connected to characters and plot so they're more likely to click the Buy button. If you find yourself explaining, clarifying, elaborating, etc., cut those sentences and move on with your life.

Exercise #3: Take the summary you wrote for Exercise #2 (if you have yet to write it, now is a fantastic time to catch up) and use the pointers you learned in this chapter to condense your plot to the bare minimum. Remove anything that seems nonessential or in the weeds.

Bonus Exercise: Surf around on Amazon, Kobo, and Apple to find descriptions that contain too much information or just the right amount. Make a mental note of ones that work particularly well, and save them for your perusal later.

Recap:

- Do not put every character, plot, and setting into your synopsis.
- Avoid using anything that requires additional explanatory sentences.
- When in doubt, save it for the book.

What's Important Enough to Include?

We've gone into some depth about what not to include in your synopses, so let's be a little more positive, shall we? Let's talk about what to include in your synopsis. Important areas to focus on for this chapter will vary from genre to genre, but there are a few things all fiction tends to need when it's summarized. First of all, you follow the journey of one, two, or at the most, three protagonists. As far as setting, plot, and theme are concerned, you're only going to note the specific areas that connect the hook of your book.

Now, you might be saying, "What the heck is my hook?"

Don't worry. In many cases "the hook" is easier to identify than you think. If someone was making a movie of your novel, what would be the one liner on the poster?

What would The Movie Trailer Guy say after speaking the words "In a world..." Your hook is the selling point that gets people excited to click the Buy button.

Here's an example. Let's say your main character is a rogue CIA agent who wants to defuse a dirty bomb. The hook of your book is probably going to revolve around an antagonist who plans to detonate the bomb in a major city, and the agent is the only man or woman who can stop it. This is a strong hook that will likely appeal to readers of the thriller genre.

If you are creating a synopsis for the book, then you might be tempted to include each clue he finds along the way as he seeks out the bomb or all of the places he stops at to find more information. But only a couple of these points actually matter or have any direct connection to the hook of "good guy vs. bad guy with a bomb." All you really need to touch upon plot-wise in this book is when the agent finds out about the bomb and where he's headed to defuse it.

Compare these two examples:

> **Bad Example:** Rowan Black is a decorated agent for the CIA. On a rare holiday from the agency, he's looking forward to catching some fish and knocking back a few cold ones. As he's reeling in a particularly stubborn mackerel, Black hears from Gary Cooper, a former informant, about a CIA cover-up of a bomb that could go off in the heart of New York City.

Fighting against his own agency, Black must battle a weapons manufacturer in Georgia. He'll need to enlist the help of an ex-wife in DC. If he can survive that long, he'll have to rely on his wits and his remaining contacts to stop his madman former handler from taking out four million people.

Good Example: Roman Black is a decorated CIA agent in need of a break. It's too bad his vacation will be short-lived. When he learns of a deep government cover-up that could end with a dirty bomb going off in Times Square, Black's only choice is to go rogue. In a race against time, Black must rely on dubious allies and former enemies to save the population of New York before it's too late.

So what did we remove from Example #1 here? First of all, we stripped the synopsis of details from his vacation, the name of his informant, and the whole business with the weapons manufacturer and his ex-wife. That information is technically all still in there, but it's been made more vague to save space and keep the synopsis focused on what's really important. We don't need to know the names of everybody and we certainly don't need to know the type of fish. These details make your prose rich, but they make your synopsis flabby and uninteresting.

Another area authors tend to go absolutely bonkers with is backstory. Authors feel as though they need to write a whole primer before a new reader comes on board. In many cases, that new reader will not make it to your first book because of the sheer amount of unnecessary info you provided up top. This information typically comes in two forms: world building and character history. I've already talked about how we don't need to know all the specific details of your fantasy or sci-fi epic, but we might even need less than you think. You may even be able to get by with half of a sentence that transitions into the good stuff: the character development portion of the synopsis. Plot and setting can be boring in a synopsis, but if you need a little bit of context for your characters, use those elements of fiction as a transition in your description.

Here are some examples of how you can use plot and setting in your synopsis transitions.

> When a planetary meltdown leaves them trapped, Eric must make a devastating choice.
>
> During the greatest war our country has ever known, Veronica and her family are persecuted for their beliefs.
>
> Fired from his third job in a row, Bernie didn't expect anything close to love.

Look at how these examples tie us right back into the character. We don't always need a lot of specifics about the intricacies of what's going on. But if your characters need a little bit of context to come alive in your synopsis, then one half of a sentence can truly work wonders. Whenever you can condense three sentences of backstory into the first half of a sentence, you get some serious brownie points from both me and your readers.

Let's talk a little bit about the character backstory portion of the program. There are so many amazing character tools out there, like character worksheets and pieces of high-end software that attach to Scrivener. They help you to figure out exactly where a character came from and what his or her objectives are in the book going forward. I think it's partly the result of these imaginative tools that has led to authors packing synopses with way too much context for our protagonists.

Much like in world building, the only information you actually need during the character setup phase must be tied back to the book's hook. If your protagonist traveling to a tropical island to serendipitously meet the girl of his dreams is important, then we may want one or half of a sentence on what drove him to the island. Let's say it's a terrible breakup that just happened with his ex-girlfriend. We don't need the name of his ex-girlfriend who just broke up with him, why they broke up, what his best friend said he should do, etc. Let's see both the positive and negative versions of this in action.

Bad Example: Patrick just bought the most beautiful engagement ring for the most incredible girl in the world. It's only when he's down on one knee that Susan Trotter tells him she's been unfaithful. He's heartbroken, but his best friend Omar has an idea that could change his life: a cruise to a tropical vacation. Miserable for the first two days, Patrick's luck changes when he spots a girl who makes his heart skip a beat. There's only one problem: she's the captain's daughter!

Good Example: Patrick had the perfect proposal all planned out, until the girl of his dreams confessed to an affair. Heartbroken and lonely, he takes a cruise to a tropical island in search of something new. When he meets Marianne, everything changes. But there's one problem: she's the ship captain's daughter!

In less than half the number of words, you've conveyed the exact same information. If you've ever heard the phrase "cut to the chase," think of the synopsis as a perpetual cutting to the chase. And the only way to get to that chase is by making a few cuts.

All right, back to the negativity! Here are a few more categories that don't quite make the "important enough" list for your synopsis:

Full Character Names

More often than not you can get by with first names alone. There is no need to inundate the reader with a middle name as well as a last name for your character. Unless he or she is a serial killer—they tend to have three names. Otherwise, I would say leave it out, and keep things as simple as possible.

More Than Two or Three Character Names

Let's say your book is based on The Hero's Journey. If that's the case, then in your story you might have the name of a hero, the name of his wife, the name of a mentor, the name of an antagonist, the name of a fool, etc. Authors have the inclination to name all these people in their descriptions, but it's a very bad instinct. I can barely remember a person's name five minutes after I've learned it. Imagine how much that process is complicated by meeting four people in quick succession. Do not litter your synopsis with a bunch of names. Stick to the protagonists and the antagonists if you have to name more than one.

More Than Two Locations

In many cases, you can get by without even mentioning where your book is taking place. If setting is important, then you may want to at least include where the main action takes place. Perhaps if you were writing a globetrotting thriller, then you'd put in more than one location. But you do not need to go overboard here. Name either the setting where the main action occurs or where the climax takes place. Do not go into too much detail here, because readers will not be able to remember just how many darn locations there are in your book.

Twice-Told Tales

This is a concept I picked up in college from one of my acting professors, Joan Darling. Twice-told tales are when you have already effectively conveyed one of the main points of your synopsis, but you go ahead and rephrase that exact thing a second time. Once you have mentioned a piece of information, there is no need to mention it again. After all, you only have a limited amount of time to get people's attention. If one character is a jerk, spend one sentence talking about how much of a douchebag he is. If a character is incredibly attractive, you've got one line to do it. Do not mention it over and over again. It's not worth it, and it's lazy writing.

Full Explanations and More Than One Specific Term for Magic Systems, Superpowers, Shifting Abilities, Etc.

I feel as though some sci-fi and fantasy authors are trying so hard to only appeal to a very specific niche of people that their synopsis involves a shopping list of crazy names of character races, species, magical abilities, and more. By using the weirdest possible names and as many of those terms as possible in their description, they will succeed at only recruiting the people who meet their strict criteria. Of course, they won't be able to pay their bills because they're not selling enough copies, but everyone has their own objectives. My objective, and what I hope is your goal as well, is to sell more books. Keep things a little bit vague and general in your description when it comes to words you've made up for your story. When you get too deep into your own terminology in a synopsis, you have to spend so much time explaining those concepts that you lose the momentum for your hook-driven plot. Just keep things simple for now. In the book you can use your 1,000 chapters to explain all of the wacky magic systems you want.

More Than One Sentence of Plot That Happens Before the Timeline of the Book

Here's another one with some serious sci-fi and fantasy offenders. Historical fiction folks, you get involved with this faux pas too. I've seen descriptions go into an entire paragraph or two about what happened 10,000 years before the plot of the book. Your reader isn't trying to learn the history of your world when she's deciding whether or not to buy your book. All she wants to do is find the next book that she is going to dive into.

Spending too much time setting up the context is going to lose you more people than you think. Save your backstory for the book itself. The description should only be about the main thrust of your story, and that means no more than one sentence of stuff that happens before the first page. I mean it.

Subplots and Side Characters

I feel like you shouldn't be too surprised about this given what I've already mentioned, but you do not need to introduce all the characters and all the plot points in your description. I think the only time where this is worth including is when you lump some of these characters or subplot into one series sentence.

Here's an example:

> To make it across the Forgotten Realm, David must battle winged gargoyles, fiery pits of fear, and a succubus who looks eerily similar to his ex-girlfriend.

Notice how we got through several of those subplots and action scenes in a single sentence. I would not spend more time than that on scenes and side plots that are contributing to the main hook of the story. If it takes too long to explain, then stick it into one of these series sentences.

Dialogue

I'm just going to say that this is my personal preference here. I've seen several authors use dialogue effectively in their descriptions. I don't think there's enough room for it unless you write the most incredible dialogue on the face of the planet. Dialogue often doesn't have context. A lack of context means you need to explain things. Explanation takes time and precious space in your short, sweet synopsis. Unless you have a very good reason for putting it in there, I'd keep the dialogue inside the book and inside the book alone.

Here's a rule of thumb when it comes to any other considerations for putting stuff in your synopsis: if you're not sure whether something belongs in there, then it most definitely doesn't belong. Take a cue from The Life-Changing Magic of Tidying Up. If a sentence won't bring your readers joy, then you should just plain throw it out.

> **Exercise #4**: Take your edited description and further cut out any additional details that fall into the categories mentioned in this chapter.
>
> **Bonus Exercise:** Write a terrible synopsis using all of the no-no's I mentioned earlier. Compare that to your edited synopsis. Assess why the concise synopsis is so much better than the load of crap you just put together.

Recap:

- All you really need to include in your synopsis are character and plot points that relate to your book's hook.
- Avoid inserting more backstory than the bare minimum.
- Do not include long character names, too many names or locations, twice-told tales, long explanations of magical plot devices, subplots, or dialogue.
- If it won't bring your readers joy, then you should leave it out.

How Do I Make It Sound Good?

You know what drives me crazy? When I write a book description for an author, and they come back to me with, let's say, over 50% of it changed. Then they asked me if I think the changes are okay. I just wonder if they can hear my exasperated sighs through the email. They should really figure out how to do that someday.

It's not that what they send me is that bad, it's just that most of them don't understand that content isn't the only thing I'm writing. I'm also writing for sound. When I write a synopsis, I write for the rhythm of the piece. Each of the sentence transitions and all of the words I pick are meant to make the book sound more appealing and for the description to flow more smoothly. I always give these authors the benefit of the doubt, of course, but when I read that description out loud,

I know that the author hasn't spoken a single word aloud. In most cases, it sounds just as choppy as the description they had in the first place.

When a synopsis fails to flow logically from idea to idea, it trips up the reader. The last thing you want to do when you're putting your description out into the world is to have it sound weird or clunky. Do you think a reader is very likely to give your book the same benefit of the doubt I have? No way. They're going to think your book sounds weird and clunky on the inside as well.

I've never quite gone into exactly what makes the sound choices I use work, but I think this chapter goes a long way toward conveying a stronger sounding synopsis in a way that's easy to apply. Here are some ways to enhance the rhythm and sound of your book's synopsis.

Vary Short Sentences and Long Sentences

I'm a big fan of William Shakespeare. In college, I only needed to take one semester with the bard to complete my English degree, but I went ahead and took three, as well as a semester abroad in Stratford-upon-Avon and Oxford. I know a lot more than the average playgoer when it comes to Romeo, Juliet, and the gang. And one thing I know is that when most people read the bard aloud, they're reading him wrong.

They tend to pause at the end of every 10-syllable

iambic pentameter line. That's not how Shakespeare is read. In his plays, you read sentences like a normal person, all the way to the punctuation. One thing that makes Shakespeare's lyricism work so well is that he mixes up shorter and longer sentences. The beauty of his variation is squandered when someone is reading one of the sonnets and every line sounds exactly the same length because of the way they mistakenly read it. It's as calming as a lullaby. This is why many people hate Shakespeare and want to go to sleep when they hear it. That and the whole 16th-17th Century language thing.

What does this have to do with your synopsis? Well, if all of the sentences in your description are just about the same length, then the reader may take in your synopsis much in the same way a middle school classroom takes in this bastardized version of Shakespeare. Every sentence starts to sound the same. They all blend together, and the words start not mattering anymore. But when you vary up the sentence length, everything in your description has more impact. You're able to highlight certain aspects of the synopsis, and you can keep the reader attentive toward what you're trying to convey.

> Erica LaPlante has lost hope. The treaty that torched her purpose may destroy everything she loves as well.
>
> Veil to the Chief by Bryan Cohen

As you can see in the above self-referential example, going with a short sentence right next to a long sentence allows you to emphasize important character points and touch upon the plot without glossing over either. Much like in Shakespeare, even a small difference between two sentences makes both stand out. Be more Shakespearian, and make sure to vary your sentence length.

End Sentences and Phrases with Harder Words

Different word origins matter. I'm not going to get too technical, but if you subscribe to the New Criticism theory of evaluating poetry and prose, then the origin of words and how they impact a piece of writing mean a lot. When you contrast much longer words of Romantic origin (i.e., Latin/Greek) with more blunt Anglo-Saxon words, you're able to play with your emphasis as well. Does that mean you're going to need to learn the roots of words and go back through the hell of learning high school vocabulary? No. I wouldn't subject you to that nightmare again. But you should just know that contrasting the words that flow (like imagination, adventure, and flourishing) with the words that don't flow (like brain, quest, and barren) can give you another tool to manipulate the sound and rhythm of your synopsis.

If you're a writer who likes to use long, flowing adjectives in your prose, just be careful that all the words in your description aren't just as long and flowing. You need to mix things up in order to keep things interesting for your readers. You may be saying to yourself, "Bryan, nobody cares about the origin of the words I use." You're right, but they can still hear the difference. They can hear when you're getting stuck in a long-winded explanation, in the same way they can hear when you're blunt.

> His plan in London is to marry the city's most beautiful debutante, and he always gets what he wants.
>
> Lord Raven by Carolyn Jewel

In the above example, the phrase "beautiful debutante" flows, while the short punchy words of "gets what he wants" make the sentence much more dynamic. If it were all short, hard words ("wed a woman with cash and land"), or only long descriptors ("and the delinquent frequently succeeds"), you wouldn't feel much momentum in the sentence at all. But because we go from longer, softer words to the blunt ones, we feel a little bit more how this character actually operates.

This advice may feel a bit too much in the weeds for some of you, but if your synopsis sounds monotonous, it may be because you need more word variety in your sentences. Mixing up the length and strength of the words might be just what you need to breathe new life into it.

Avoid Repeating Yourself

Authors have a tendency to be a little impatient when they write a synopsis. The great care they take toward varying their word choice within their books doesn't always translate to marketing materials like the synopsis. While the thesaurus may be close at hand when you're working on Chapter 1, it might remain on the shelf when you're putting together the blurb. I see too many descriptions where the same adjective is used twice in a single paragraph. I've even seen it where the same word is used twice in back-to-back sentences. A reader probably isn't going to think this is lazy (even though I do), but it certainly doesn't sound very good.

I recommend that you avoid repeating yourself unless it is for some kind of effect. In many cases, it's a bad idea, but every so often it can work well for you.

> Little does he know he's headed into something much more dangerous. Something that could leave both of them and their secrets laid to rest.
>
> Freefall by Carolyn Jewel

> Doctor Kincaid has a secret. A secret that could kill Kaci. A secret that could wipe out what's left of the human race.
>
> Recycling Humanity by Heather Lee Dyer

In the first example, "something" is used twice to enhance the vague descriptor that serves as a cliffhanger in this synopsis. Whatever the something is, it's not only more dangerous, but it could kill the main characters. That's one heck of a something, and that is one of the few situations where repetition works.

In the second example, we get to use "secret" three times for effect. Not only does the bad guy have a secret, and not only could it kill our main character, but it could destroy humanity too. That may be a secret that's worth repeating three times. But unless you're using this kind of parallel construction in your description, I do not recommend using repetition in your synopsis. Find new words to keep the reader from getting tripped up while reading your summary.

Trade Out Boring Words to Enhance Emotional Impact

Some words simply have more emotional impact than others. Compare "affection" with "passion," and "ruler" with "tyrant." Sometimes a synonym of a word, or a stronger form of that word, can make the difference between your book sounding exciting and sounding bland. Author Robert Scanlon once told me that some words are more semantically-charged than others. That means there's more meaning behind them, and they inspire a different kind of reaction than normal words. These words can really vary from genre to genre.

"Passion" will obviously be a key word in romance or any book with a romantic subplot. A strong word in a thriller might be "annihilation" or "apocalypse." Mystery will use the word "murder." Dark fantasy or horror might emphasize the word "soul." The list of semantically-charged words that you could use for your genre is probably too long to put here. But if you know your genre well enough, you likely know the buzzwords—the words that get your particular brand of readers excited to read that genre. If you use the words with the greatest possible impact, then you're more likely to get people fired up to click the Buy button.

The best place to put these semantically-charged words is at the end of your sentences, particularly toward the end of your paragraphs. You can also use a blunt Anglo-Saxon word in these locations as well. By using a word with more oomph at the key transitional points in your synopsis, it gives you just enough of a stop-and-pause moment to keep the momentum as you transition to the next paragraph while still keeping the attention of the reader. This doesn't mean you can't use emotionally-impactful language throughout, but it's especially important that you use this kind of language when you're trying to keep hold of the reader as you make a leap from one idea to the next.

Hearing Your Synopsis Loud and Clear

I ask all the authors I work with to read their descriptions aloud to make sure it sounds as good as humanly possible. How many of them do you think actually do it? I would guess about 25%. That makes me a little sad, but I understand that people are busy and they don't necessarily like speaking aloud, especially when they can sit in their writer chair in silence all day long instead.

This is one of those situations where you need to make a sound. It's the only way to know if your word choice is effective. It's the best method for hearing how the rhythm is working, if you need to vary sentence length, and if you've accidentally repeated a word. The best authors know that saying their words out loud is the only way to ensure their prose passes the test. Please do the same thing for your synopsis.

When the rhythm is working in your favor, momentum continues from the beginning sentence all the way until the end. What you write should be like a snowball rolling down a mountain and causing a very positive avalanche. In the next chapter, we'll go into a few more ways to preserve that momentum so that your reader goes from your hook to your summary to the Buy button.

> **Exercise #5:** Experiment on your existing synopsis by varying the sentence length, ending sentences with harder words, removing all repetition, and inserting in semantically-charged words. Once you've done this, read your new description aloud and make any changes necessary.

> **Bonus Exercise:** Make a stream of consciousness list of the words that have the most emotional impact in your genre. Keep this list handy for whenever you're writing a synopsis in the future.

Recap:

- Clunky descriptions cause readers to stop reading.
- Vary short sentences and long sentences to avoid lulling readers to sleep.
- End sentences and paragraphs with harder words or words with more emotional impact.
- Avoid using repetition unless your synopsis includes parallel construction.
- Read your synopsis aloud to ensure it sounds like a winner.

How Do I Make My Synopsis Grow From Beginning to End?

Like most fiction, the synopsis has a tendency to lag in the middle. One of the problems with this low-energy midpoint is that prospective readers may not have the attention span to read enough of your drooping synopsis to be willing to click the Buy button. The best way to solve this is by not having any slow spots in your description. You want your blurb to have momentum throughout the short piece, taking your daredevil reader up the ramp, all the way across the chasm, and safely to the other side where they can start reading your book.

Some of the sound and rhythm suggestions from the previous chapter will help you keep up the pace. Here are a few more that will hone your synopsis to a sharp point. By the time I'm through with you, your synopsis will be brutally efficient at getting readers to take action.

Trim Phrases That Slow Down the Reader

When you rephrase part of your synopsis, those new words do not always need to be the same exact length. In fact, when you're revising your blurb, you should always be willing to trade down. It's basically one of the tenets of copywriting to put your ideas into fewer words. Why say something in 10 words, when you can say it in five? Having fewer words allows for more momentum and impact in your description. Always be willing to trade five for three, four for three, three for two, etc. Every word counts.

> **Bad Example:**
>
> Maddie Winters has never been in a long-term relationship.
>
> **Good Example:**
> Maddie Winters isn't big on relationships.
> My Demon Warlord by Carolyn Jewel

In the above example, we've made a trade of nine words for six words. Not only have we gotten rid of three pesky words, but the second example is tighter and has more emotional impact and a cool style to it. Always look through your description to find areas where you can use slightly different words to condense your sentences. This is particularly effective if you're looking to vary sentence length. Making these trades is like trading your apple for a piece of candy at elementary school lunch. You always take the candy.

Remove Confusing Explanations

We often don't make things simple on ourselves. Sometimes we authors write long and convoluted books, which lead to long, convoluted synopses. In a book, we have the opportunity to explain away detailed world building, magic systems, and breathtaking locations. We don't have that luxury in a synopsis, so we often mention confusing subjects without having the time or space to explain them. Making our readers work when they try to read our descriptions is a recipe for disaster. Every reader should be able to understand the basics of your book inside your blurbs. If they don't, it means that you've made a mistake. The onus is on you, not them.

The best way to determine if your description contains something confusing on the inside is to present it to a general audience of readers or authors. If more than 20% of respondents have no freaking clue what's going on in your plot, it means you're not being clear enough. Often, you can get away with something a little confusing if you shake it up a bit. Take out some of the specific names and places, and make them more general and understandable. Inside the book, you can elucidate these topics. For now, remove the confusing bits and keep the momentum flowing.

Connect All Your Sentences

Earlier in the book, I mentioned how transitions at the beginning of sentences worked as a strong way to include plot without bogging down the synopsis. That's just one use of these helpful tools within your blurbs. Transitioning from one sentence to the next is a prime way to keep momentum strong within your piece. Transition phrases often start with words like "when," "after," "as," "before," "with," and a series of others. If your description sounds clunky, then you probably need to use more transitional phrases between your sentences to keep things going. I think it's a good rule of thumb to use one of these transitions at least once in every three sentences of your synopsis. Typically, that sentence would be the middle of the three.

Employ the Quick Twist

The quick twist is a term I've come up with for a certain tactic I've seen used very effectively in descriptions. This phenomenon occurs when something good or neutral is happening in one sentence before it very quickly turns into something dangerous or negative. The quick twist is a strong way to explain consequences or circumstances in your synopsis without using a long-winded explanation. It helps to build tension in your blurb without having to do too much linguistically. Here's an example:

> His success should be the pinnacle of his career. He never expected it to threaten his life.
>
> The Algorithm by CL Walker

Neither of these sentences is very long. They don't have too many specifics inside, but you have a positive sentiment followed by a bit of a twist. When you can provide a reader with the unexpected, even in a short 200-word blurb, you might just inspire them to click the Buy button as well. Note here that the semantically-charged words of "career" and "life" end both of those sentences. "Success" and "threats" also carry a fair bit of weight.

Another use of the quick twist is to introduce a villain or a conflict. I'm a big fan of using the quick twist in the third sentence of the first paragraph of a synopsis, once I've established the opening stakes for a character. I also love using it at the end of the synopsis, once the tension has been ratcheted up as high as possible.

> Someone wants the data John stole, and he's willing to kill to get it.
>
> The Algorithm by CL Walker

In this case, we've taken a neutral plot point and twisted it around to the main conflict of the piece. It's a great use of the space in your description, especially if you're trying to wring a lot of emotion from just one or two sentences at the end. It conveys a significant amount of information in a short period of time, keeping the reader on the edge of his or her seat.

Grow the Tension Throughout Your Sentences

This isn't a complicated tip. If you're using transitions at the beginning of your sentences to throw in a few plot points or setting notes, then the end of your sentence should demonstrate how the character and the conflict interact. Long story short, you show your characters running into trouble. As you get deeper into your synopsis, you want readers to see that your characters are in danger of failing their mission, missing out on love, or (my favorite choice) dying. These tension-rich moments should increase as your description works its way to the end.

The best way to build excitement throughout your synopsis is to make more exciting things happen as your synopsis grows to a close. The last few sentences of your summary are not meant for introducing new characters or explaining complicated aspects of the plot. You need tension. You need to put your characters in danger of not getting what they want. The more you do that as you get toward the end of your blurb, the more likely readers are to get excited and take action.

End With a Cliffhanger

The best way to take that logical tension all the way to its boiling point at the end of a synopsis is to close things out with a cliffhanger. What better way to get readers to want to learn what happens in the book then by forcing them to read the book to figure out what happens? This is so important that I've devoted an entire chapter to ending your synopsis with a "cliffhanger for the ages." After you've done the exercise at the bottom of this chapter, feel free to move onto the edge of that treacherous mountain.

> **Exercise #6:** Apply the tips from this chapter into your existing synopsis. Trade longer phrases for shorter phrases, search for any confusing plot points that you can remove, add at least one transition to each set of three sentences, employ the quick twist when appropriate, and ensure that more tension-filled moments show up in the last few sentences of your synopsis. Make sure to read your description out loud one more time, just to ensure that your changes haven't added any errors.
>
> **Bonus Exercise:** Write out 10 quick twists you could use in the synopses for future books that you plan on writing.

Recap:

- Most synopses lag in the middle, so you have to take action to keep the momentum going.
- Trade out longer phrases for shorter ones.
- Excise any confusing plot points and save them for the book.
- Use one transition at least once every three sentences.
- Employ the "quick twist" to build excitement.
- Save the biggest moments of your synopsis for the end.
- Finish off your synopsis with a cliffhanger.

How Do I End Things with a Bang?

I think I have an idea why so many authors end synopses with a whimper, not a bang. Most authors who write these things run out of patience and say to themselves, "Please get this thing off my plate!" At that exact moment, these worldly scribes publish their synopsis as is and begin working on the next book in their production calendar. That's the only logical explanation I can come up with for why so many of these blurbs just sort of end with no big "buy-worthy" moment. People, we have to do better. I know we can do better. And the best way to end our synopses in such a way that the reader feels compelled to download the book and read the rest of our series is to use an epic cliffhanger.

Here are three reasons why you need a cliffhanger at the end of your synopsis:

1. When you have a cliffhanger, readers want to know what happens next. To accomplish this, they buy your book.
2. If the reader isn't invested in your character and seeing that person in danger, then they're not your ideal reader anyway. In that way, cliffhangers do a better job of getting your target readers on board.
3. Having a reader end your synopsis by saying, "Ooh, that's interesting," as opposed to murmuring, "Meh," is always a good thing.

One of your jobs as the author of a synopsis is to take your readers to the highest possible point of the mountain. You need to burn the bridges behind them and leave them at the edge of the cliff. You need to put your character in a seemingly impossible situation where everything seems to be against him or her from falling in love, killing the bad guy, saving the world, etc. And that's when you end things. Doing anything less will decrease your number of sales.

Note: Cliffhangers get a bad rap for ending books without satisfying readers. I'm not so convinced they're bad at the end of series novels, but whatever your opinion is using these important devices inside your books, you need to use them in your description. It significantly increases the chances that a reader will be interested enough to click the Buy button.

Here are a series of cliffhangers and my explanations for why they work well:

> Chris may hold more cards than he thinks in a game that puts his life on the line.
>
> The City by CL Walker

You might be surprised that I'm not starting off here with a "slam bang" end of the world example. That's because I want you to know that not all cliffhangers need to have the literal person-dangling-from-a-cliff scenario. Sure, we do say that the main character's life is on the line in this situation, but we add another wrinkle here. We learn the main character may also have a little more information than he realized. He might have some kind of special skill or he's a stronger fighter or negotiator than he supposed. This gives us a lot of information in a short period of time and conveys that the main character is in grave danger. It's subtle, but effective.

> Black has one chance to keep Ramsey behind bars, and it will be the toughest fight of her career.
>
> Burnout by Larry A. Winters

Here's another one that doesn't end with the apocalypse, but it does raise the stakes to their highest possible point. The lawyer in question has only one opportunity to achieve her objective of keeping a criminal in prison. It doesn't get to be a much bigger deal for a lawyer in that situation. We also get to see from this example that her goal is going to be incredibly challenging. It's also assumed that she has no idea how she's going to pull it off. We may not have death or the fate of humanity in the balance on this one, but we have made the reader wonder how the protagonist is going to achieve her objective. And that's a very good thing.

> How she handles the sins of the past may control her future...
>
> The Perfect Story by Heather Lee Dyer

Oh, man. I love cliffhangers like this. You don't need to read this cliffhanger in context to see just how much is going on in the story. The protagonist is dealing with some awful things that happened in the past, but when she gets control of them, her whole world may change. I'm also a big fan of the ellipsis at the end of this because it literally leaves the reader hanging. You can achieve the same kind of dangling moment with a question mark at the end, as we'll see in the next example.

> After pasts riddled with pain, can Darcy and Marcus let themselves love again?
>
> Mistress by Blackmail by Caro LeFever

Here we get a romance example. We have a nice transition right at the top of things that speeds up the momentum of the sentence. Then we have our two lovebirds coping with what has previously happened, as we wonder if they can allow themselves to love each other. This is the apocalypse version of romance. We don't have anybody dying, but the reader is dying to know if the two characters will get together. Pretty much all romance synopses should end with some kind of question being posed as to whether or not the characters will survive together. It doesn't have to be a question per se, but readers need to be concerned enough to click the Buy button to find out.

> Even at the top of her game, Alex may not make it out of this one alive.
>
> Invisible Journey by Mary Buckham

Now here's a pretty traditional cliffhanger. We've got a badass paranormal heroine who is pretty great at beating the bad guys. This is not the first book in a series, so we know that Alex has made it out of sticky situations before. She's at the top of her game, after all. But in order to keep our readers excited, they need to assume that Alex might not survive. I can tell you right now, she probably will, but this is the way to go with long-standing series when you are putting the same main character in danger over and over again. Readers need to know that the danger is real and that it might have consequences.

> But when they find out the truth, they'll need to make a choice that will change their lives forever.
>
> Protect Us by R. A. Roque

If you've ever listened to my author podcast with Robert Scanlon called *The Split*, we found that most young adult novels are more successful when they have some kind of mystery baked into the plot. In fact, I feel as though most books do well to have some kind of mystery spurring the readers on toward the finish. This is an example of a cliffhanger where you learn the main characters will find out the truth of the main plot mystery. And when they find out that truth, everything will transform for them. That leaves the reader wanting to figure out the truth, and how the protagonists lives will change afterwards. It's like a double mystery that your reader is more than willing to buy the book in order to solve.

> She's the answer to a thousand-year-old legend, and he might just be falling for her...
>
> The Tarczal Alliance by J. Paulette Forshey

We've got a combination of a few cliffhanger tactics in this one. First of all, we have the plot point transition at the beginning of the sentence. We also have the romance convention of the guy possibly falling for the girl. And we have the literal cliffhanger of the ellipsis. This classic cliffhanger works well for paranormal romance type books, because we're getting a bit of the supernatural as well as a bit of the attraction. We also happen to have the mysterious inclusion of the thousand-year-old legend. There's a lot going on here, but it's not overwhelming for the reader because it's not all that detailed. We don't have to learn the name of the legend or the intricacies of the prophecy. All we need to know about the legend is how the guy might be falling for the gal who fulfills it. You can do a lot in a short period of time with a small number of words.

I wanted to show you a couple of cliffhangers for some middle grade/children's books as well. In these books, the stakes are very different compared to other genres where life is often hanging in the balance. Usually, you're not ending one of these descriptions with someone dying because the parents aren't going to be as interested in buying the book for their child. But that doesn't mean you still can't use the cliffhanger concept.

> The young wizards in training must combat the evil of the Hourglass or the world as they know it will be consumed by darkness.
>
> The Rock and the Rainbow Serpent by Vicki McGahey

There's no reason you can't use a substitution for the world ending that doesn't quite sound as bad as a deadly apocalypse. The world being "consumed by darkness" isn't nearly as rough as the human race being exterminated or the world ending, but it still sounds creepy and will make an impact on either the young adult checking out the synopsis or the parent buying the book.

> Can Wooly convince Butterscotch to give friendship a try?
>
> Wooly Meets the Chickens by Suzanne Blumer

This example may feel a bit trite when compared to high-stakes espionage and thousand-year-old legends from earlier, but high stakes are different depending on the context of the book. If you have something cute with a moral at the end, possibly in a book that's illustrated, then your cliffhanger needs to fit what that book is conveying. In this case, you have a dog and some chickens. That's what's happening in the book. You have a dog trying to make friends with some chickens. Those are the lowish stakes of the story, but we still want to leave the potential readers with the question of whether or not it's going to happen. Cliffhangers work no matter what genre you're in. Use them in every description that you write. It's the only thing that's guaranteed to leave the reader wanting more.

Exercise #7: Take your existing synopsis and add a relevant cliffhanger to the end.

Bonus Exercise: Write 10 cliffhangers for books you have written or books you have read. Make sure these cliffhangers would work in the context of a synopsis.

Recap:

- Cliffhangers leave the reader wanting more, which prompts him or her to buy.
- End things when the character is in danger of not achieving his or her goal.
- By using the right mix of vague and specific terms, you can convey a great deal of information with a concise cliffhanger.
- Using an ellipsis or a question mark is a prime way to end your cliffhanger.
- Even middle grade/children's books can end with their own sort of cliffhanger to get the parents or children excited.

What's a Step-by-Step System I Can Use for My Synopsis?

If you're impatient like me, it's likely that you skipped through the first seven chapters of this book just so you could get to the good stuff. If that's the case, then welcome to the book! But I have to say, there's a lot of important detail earlier in this book that will make the step-by-step system in this chapter make a lot more sense. This isn't that long of a book, so I think it's in your best interest to go back to the first seven chapters and learn the context behind the steps in this chapter. I can't force you to do anything, but if I could, I'd make sure you read those first seven chapters and complete the exercises. Now I'm stepping off my soapbox and back onto my treadmill desk.

In this chapter, I've laid out seven steps you can take to write a clickable, tension-filled synopsis. By no means is this the only way to summarize the plot and character arcs in your book. I even considered not including this chapter, because I don't want everyone to just copy the same formula and use it over and over again. But I know these kinds of things are very helpful, so use this seven-step process below to write your synopsis. Just please give yourself a little bit of leeway to change things up as you see them. There is never one right way to do things. All I ask is that you keep that in mind.

The Synopsis Writing System

1. Introduce the main character

First and foremost, you're going to introduce your protagonist by name and include one small detail about him or her. This isn't the time for a three-part complex sentence. You don't need to pack all the info in at once. Just introduce the character and include one relevant detail.

> **Example:** Ted Finley was your typical wise-cracking teenager.

2. Establish the beginning stakes for the character

Over the course of the following sentence or two, write what's going on with the character at the beginning of the book. Once again, you don't need to overcomplicate things. Even in an intricate fantasy novel, you don't need to mention the five kingdoms by name, or all of the conflicts going on in the outer realms. Just say what's going on as it affects this main character. Don't worry, we'll get into what happens if you have multiple characters in just a second.

> **Example:** After a harrowing breakup, an otherworldly force gave him abilities beyond his wildest dreams.

3. Escalate the tension for the character

Here's where the magic happens. Through reading the earlier chapters in this book, you have all sorts of tools at your disposal to start ratcheting up the excitement as it pertains to the main character's circumstances. You can use a quick twist to show how his life transitions from boring to dangerous. You can use hard or semantically-charged words at the end of a sentence for emphasis. This is the time to start thinking about how you can best convey the conflict of the story through your character's circumstances.

> **Example:** When he accidentally displays his powers for the world to see, Ted becomes an instant celebrity and the target of a gang of undead thugs.

4. Repeat steps 1-3 for additional main characters

If you only have one protagonist in your story, then you

can skip this step. If you have more than one, this is your opportunity to essentially replicate what you did in steps one through three with the other character(s). Once again, keep things simple. There's no need to overwhelm the reader with too much information.

> **Example:** Sixteen-year-old Erica LaPlante was six-feet-under when a blast of blue light brought her body back to life. Armed with the consciousness of a fierce warrior, Erica must keep her teenage urges at bay to protect the newfound hero.

5. Bring the characters together

This is probably the shortest step in the entire process, because it doesn't even need to take an entire sentence. We have a tendency as authors to want to dive deep into the scenes where our characters connect. We want to convey all of the emotions and the circumstances that brought them into the same place, but we don't need to do all of that in a description. That's what the book is for, so let's just cut to the chase.

> **Example:** When sparks fly between Ted and Erica, (...)

6. Raise the stakes even higher for the character(s)

We've got our characters established. Check. Our characters are now in the same place. Check. Now, we need to bring the tension up to a simmer. This step may involve hinting at the main villain or the endgame for our characters.

> **Example:** (...), Erica wants nothing more than to hide who she really is and the dangerous mission they must face.

7. Put the character(s) in the ultimate danger of failing, dying, not falling in love, etc.

This step is really going to differ between genres. If it's romance, then you might hint at the characters not getting together. If it's a mystery, then you might talk about the characters becoming the killer's next victim. If it's a children's book, then you might talk about the dog and chicken not getting along. No matter what your genre, you're showing the main characters in danger of not achieving their main goal. This is your cliffhanger.

> **Example:** But after their school comes under attack, Ted and Erica must use everything at their disposal to save their friends, the town, and... well, the world.

You can adapt this system in whatever way you like. Not all steps are going to be just one or two sentences. Some steps might be even shorter depending on if you have multiple protagonists. I'd like you to think of these seven steps as more of a guideline for writing a synopsis that gets readers excited to put the book on their e-reader.

In the next chapter, we'll discuss a different seven-step system (what's with this guy and 7s?) for editing the synopsis you've just written.

> **Exercise #8:** Rewrite your description from scratch using the system above.
>
> **Bonus Exercise:** Create a new description from scratch using the steps above for the next book on your production calendar. If you don't have a book planned, just make one up.

Recap:

1. Introduce the main character.
2. Establish the beginning stakes for the character.
3. Escalate the tension for the character.
4. Repeat steps 1-3 for additional main characters.
5. Bring the characters together.
6. Raise the stakes even higher for the character(s).
7. Put the character(s) in the ultimate danger of failing, dying, not falling in love, etc.

How Do I Edit My Synopsis Down to the Essential?

You've got your incredible synopsis ready for a healthy dose of self-editing. Now that you have those couple of paragraphs primed for maximum emotional impact, it's time to increase that tension through the use of sound, rhythm, and momentum. Let's get to it.

The Synopsis Editing System

1. Simplify your synopsis as much as possible

Have you explained a plot point in three sentences that can be turned into two? Do you spend a whole sentence without mentioning a character that could be turned into a transitional phrase? This step is for distilling what you've written into the essential by keeping everything simple.

Go through your synopsis with a fine-toothed comb and look for ways that you can trim out unnecessary plots or explanations that you could save for the book. As I've mentioned before, rewriting a specific plot point or character in a way that's more vague or general can drastically decrease your word count.

2. Trade down your words

Have you written something in six words where you could've used four? Has your verbosity increased the word count of your description by 20% or more? This is your opportunity to fix those problems. Look for ways throughout your synopsis to turn five words into three, or nine into six, or any other way to use different phrasing or language to make your synopsis shorter. You may have to use different words or a slightly different order in your sentences to make them shorter. Step two can be a little bit stressful if you're the kind of person who writes long, complex sentences. But in almost 99% of cases, it's much better to say something in a less flowery way to save on your number of words.

Imagine that you're a Bizarro Charles Dickens who is paid more if you use fewer words. It's one of those situations where less is more. When you trade down in words throughout your synopsis, you'll give each individual word a lot more impact. Apropos of nothing, Bizarro Charles Dickens would make an awesome villain.

3. Remove any phrases that will slow the reader down

Explanations of plot and introducing additional characters can force readers to process information instead of enjoying the story that you're telling. There are a couple of options for getting rid of these. Sometimes you can just plain cut them and pretend they never existed. If they're completely necessary, then you can turn them into transitions that will keep the momentum of your synopsis going forward. Whichever you choose, remember that your main objective is not to explain the plot. Your goal should be to evoke emotional reactions from your reader.

> **Bad Example:** The Order began the systematic removal of all people with the power to heal. David's family was one of the first targets. They hid from the government for over a century.
>
> **Good Example:** After the Order rounded up all the healers, David's family went into hiding to avoid persecution.

Don't worry about losing a little bit of information during your edit. The only person who thought that information was necessary was you. You're not the one buying your book. Practice the art of selflessness by thinking about your readers.

4. Read your synopsis aloud and look for areas that need additional emotional impact

It's time to start applying some of the tips from Chapter 5 to adjust how your synopsis sounds. Do you end your paragraphs with short, hard, or semantically-charged words? If not, this is the step to start putting those tips into practice. Have you avoided using repetition (except for effect)? It's much easier to hear that you've used the same word twice while you read it aloud. Are all of your sentences the same length or do you vary it up for more impact?

Reading the description to yourself gives you the opportunity to hear if all the sentences sound mostly the same. You may have unintentionally placed emphasis in the same exact spot in each sentence, or it might just sound like you're reading Shakespeare line by line without worrying about punctuation. Remember to vary things up by interchanging shorter sentences with longer sentences, particularly when you need to bring attention to an important point in the shorter sentence. I recommend having the tips from Chapter 5 open in one window while you have your synopsis document open in the other window. I'm a big fan of split screens for this sort of work.

5. Ensure that you end with a bang

When you work on this step, you need to pay attention to the last two sentences in your synopsis. You'll need to make sure that you're building the stakes and raising them up until you get to the cliffhanger. Do the last two lines move readers to the edge of their seat, or are they just going to get up and go to the bathroom? Take your synopsis to the summit of excitement. Readers need to know that there is some compelling reason for them to pick up the book. That reason makes them care if the characters are going to fall in love, save the world, or escape from the insane lunatic. Leave readers wondering about the resolution of your book's main conflict. Present it in the most emotional, high-stakes way possible. And then leave them at the edge of the cliff, forcing them to buy the book to find out what happens next.

6. Get feedback and take it with a grain of salt

I realize that taking criticism is hard. First of all, it makes you feel as though your writing is somehow inadequate. Secondly, everybody has an opinion. If you ask enough people then you'll get contradicting feedback on every single line in your synopsis. But, much in the way that you take feedback from beta readers for a critique group, if the same point comes up over and over again, then you know it probably needs your attention. When only one person brings up a tiny issue, then you may not need to tackle it at all.

I recommend that you ask your readers and anyone who loves your particular genre for their feedback first. They are the ones who you want to provoke an emotional reaction in, so their opinion is by far the most important.

If you need additional feedback, then you can bring it into my free Selling for Authors Facebook Group, which has over 1,500 authors who can help you in your efforts. Click here to ask to join. Simply take the synopsis you have, copy and paste it in the group, and wait for people to respond.

Make any changes that seem to come up in a lot of your critical feedback, and then go back through steps 1-6 to ensure the new things you've written pass the editing system. Going through the editing checklist a second time helps you to make sure that the new lines "sound good" and provide your readers with the strongest possible emotional impact.

7. Read it aloud one more time and post it!

If you've gone through every step in chapter 8 and chapter 9, then one more reading should be all you need to make sure you've avoided any errors or anything that lacks the pop you desire. It's time to let your duckling fly away into the cloudless sky.

Some of the authors I've worked with simply needed to change their book description to see a boost in sales. That's not always the case. I always recommend that authors use some kind of promotion to send additional traffic to their sales pages after they've made the change. This ensures that more eyeballs get to see the new synopsis you've put out there, which can lead to a significantly higher percentage of buyers. If you don't raise your traffic much, then you may not see all that much of a spike. Content is just one part of the puzzle.

Feel free to use Facebook ads, Amazon Marketing Services ads (a.k.a. KDP Select ads), free discount promos through sites like Bargain Booksy, BookBub, and eReaderNewsToday, and group promos like Multi-Author Facebook Events.

You and your synopsis have been through quite a journey together. I'm excited for you to put out the most sizzling version of your synopsis possible. In the next chapter, I'll go into a few additional considerations you may have for your synopsis, including where you put it, and how long it should be.

> **Exercise #9:** Use the checklist from this chapter to edit your synopsis. This may take a few days, since it requires that you get feedback from other readers and authors before you finish. Rome wasn't built in a day.
>
> **Bonus Exercise:** Use the editing checklist to help another author improve his or her synopsis. You can use the Selling for Authors Facebook Group to find book descriptions that need your critical assistance.

Recap:
1. Simplify your synopsis as much as possible.
2. Trade down your words.
3. Remove any phrases that will slow the reader down.
4. Read your synopsis aloud and look for areas that need additional emotional impact.
5. Ensure that you end with a bang.
6. Get feedback and take it with a grain of salt.
7. Read it aloud one more time and post it!

How Long Should My Synopsis Be, Where Should I Use It, and Other Common Considerations

You've finished a brilliant work of art. I hope by this point you realize that the synopsis is not just something you have to do. It's an expression of your creativity. Much like your prose, you're trying to entertain people and give them either an escape or something to get excited about. Your synopsis can serve that purpose too. Now you have all the tools necessary to make it happen with all of your synopses in the future.

Isn't that great? I think it's great.

Here are a few additional considerations you might have when it comes to your synopsis.

Where Do I Put It?

I mentioned earlier in the book that I don't think you need a separate synopsis for your back cover copy or a different paperback description compared to your digital version. I feel like they can all be the same. We're living in a digital world, people. Most people are choosing to buy from your product description on Kobo, Amazon, Apple, and the other retailers. If you do sell a lot of paperbacks, I say just use the same description as you created in this book. Remember that KDP and CreateSpace have different formatting when you post them (more on formatting in a sec).

The only time you'll probably need to change or condense something is when you submit to a deal site like Bargain Booksy that requires a description of a small number of characters (i.e., 100-200). In those cases, just take your hook and your cliffhanger, put them into the required space, and be done with it. That's it. All you need to do is copy and paste your book's hook and the cliffhanger from the end of your synopsis.

Trying to condense all the rhythm and awesomeness that you've just developed into that short of a space may blow up your brain when you're already trying to make your promotion work. It's much better to just grab portions from what you've already written and call it a day. In many cases, readers won't make their final decision until they've reached your sales page anyway. And that's where you'll have your full synopsis in view to get readers fired up.

How Long Should It Be?

Ugh. I guess I can't just write "I don't care and it doesn't matter" here since everybody always asks how long their synopsis should be. Look, it's probably going to be under 300 words. Maybe even under 200. What's much more important than the length of your synopsis is the sound and the emotional impact. If you've gone through the entire process and used the step-by-step checklist in chapters 8 and 9, then you should be completely set when it comes to word count.

If prospective readers or fellow authors say that your description feels too long, then you've got work to do. You'll need to condense things further, no matter how many words it actually is. The feel of your synopsis is much more important than fulfilling some ideal word count. If it feels too long, then it's too long.

How Do I Format My Description?

This is pretty simple on the non-Amazon retailers. Copy and paste what you've got and then bold and italicize anything that needs it using each site's formatting tools. On Amazon, you can leave things as they are or you can insert some HTML coding in the appropriate spots. I personally use Author Marketing Club's Description Tool to format all of my descriptions and the descriptions of my clients. But there's something you need to keep in mind, and that is how your synopsis shows up differently on desktop vs. mobile.

The way your synopsis is displayed on different devices has changed multiple times even just in the last year, and it will probably change many times in the future. Currently, you see about 3-4 lines on the desktop version of your synopsis before you have to click a button to see more. On mobile, you see about those same 3 to 4 lines of text, but they aren't formatted. When you click on the description, the text shows up on a new page with any formatting code or bolded portions you've inserted. And like I mentioned earlier, Amazon CreateSpace has a different set of formatting tools as well.

Regardless of how you format your synopsis, it's best to start things off strong, because you have a limited amount of time to make an impact. Truth be told, you could probably get away without much formatting at all. If you want to take things to another level, play around with the existing description tools out there and see if it makes an impact on your sales. You should always test to see how small changes like this affect your bottom line.

How Can I Use This Synopsis to Get Traditionally Published?

I've been told that a synopsis is a key part of your query letter to agents and/or publishing houses. This version of the synopsis is more of the one-page variety, not so much the system that I've conveyed in this book. Does that mean you can't use aspects of my process in creating a more compelling and exciting version of your book summary? Of course you can. Take this system and apply it to your query letter as much as possible. The people who will be reading your books on the slush pile will be happy to hear something that actually sounds emotionally compelling. Can I promise that applying this process is more likely to get your book picked up so that you can get the six-figure advance you're waiting for? I definitely cannot promise anything like that. My expertise is in self-publishing, not the traditional world.

That being said, I think that anyone who is trying to be traditionally published these days should also have their fingers in the self-publishing pie. Traditional publishing takes a long time to recognize author potential. If you feel as though you have that potential, then by all means put out those query letters, but I'm a big fan of diversification. Self-publishing is a much quicker path to getting your books in the hands of readers. Using a synopsis like the one I've described in this book will only help you to get more books into the hands of even more readers. Keep all this in mind when you make your decision of how you want to publish, but writing a description that gets more people excited will never hurt you in this business.

Should I Put Anything Else in My Description Other Than Just the Synopsis?

I told you at the start of the book I have a very particular way of writing descriptions, but I didn't want to force your hand to do it my way. If you're interested in writing more than just a synopsis in an effort to guide readers to additional sales, then check out the next chapter for more info on my four-part description system.

> **Exercise #10:** If you have yet to post your new synopsis to the sales page of your choice, go ahead and do it right now without worrying about the length or the formatting. It's time to take action. Stop messing around and get to work.

Recap:
- Your synopsis goes on e-retailers like Kobo, Amazon, and Apple.
- It can be the same on any platform and your back cover without changes.
- To shorten your synopsis for discount marketing promotions, use the hook and the cliffhanger.
- Length is much less important than how long your description "feels."
- Don't worry about formatting at first, but there are tools you can use to format on Amazon (like the one on Author Marketing Club).

- Feel free to use this system on query letters, but there are no guarantees this system will get you traditionally published.
- Read the next chapter to learn what else goes into the description.

What Else Goes Into the Description?

Much like I recommend in your synopsis, this book is going to end with a little bit of a cliffhanger. I know, I know. You're on the edge of your seat.

I consider the synopsis a very important part of my four-part description system. Here's a rough outline of what my system looks like:

1. Tagline
2. Synopsis
3. Selling Paragraph
4. Call to Action

Tagline

The tagline (also known as a headline or logline) is essentially the hook of your piece condensed into one punchy line. It's the movie poster catch phrase. It's the elevator pitch you make when you tell people about your book. Statistics show that 80% of people stop reading your copywriting after the first line. Your tagline is the effort to keep people reading the rest. Having a strong tagline in place ensures that no matter how much of your description displays on desktop or mobile devices, readers will want to read more.

Synopsis

I hope you didn't skip ahead, because we already went over this in great detail. The synopsis essentially elaborates on the hook that was just posted in the tagline. It flows, it grows, and it shows exactly why prospective readers will love this book. See Chapters 1-10 for more info.

The Selling Paragraph

Once you've got readers excited about your characters and plot, now comes the time for reeling them in. The selling paragraph reasserts what the book is by explaining the genre, where it is in the series, etc. It also tells readers why they will like your book. This section includes the author's name and peppy adjectives that readers of the genre will identify with. The selling paragraph is meant to break down barriers that potential readers have toward picking up your book. If they know and like your genre and the adjectives you use sound appealing to them, they are much more likely to click through to the sale.

Call to Action (CTA)

This is how all book descriptions should end. In the CTA you give the reader a command explaining what they should do now that they've finished your description. Usually this is in the form of telling them to buy the book, tap a certain button, or download it on Kindle Unlimited. Calls to action are known to be effective in ads and sales pitches, and you need one at the end of your description.

Speaking of CTAs... would you like to find out more about the four-part description system, as well as the other major areas of author copywriting like emails to readers, Facebook ads, and landing pages? I hope you just said "yes" out loud.

Go to www.sellingforauthors.com to download a free cheat sheet on the four-part description system. You will also get a free mini-course on writing emails that will take your author career to the next level.

Closing Up Shop

I'm afraid we've come to the end, my friends. I love teaching in all of its forms. As a teacher, you have the satisfying opportunity to share information that you've picked up along the way. You get to save so many people time and energy trying to go through all the trial and error that you went through on your own. It truly is an amazing thing that I'm so lucky to have the opportunity to do. Thank you for that.

You'll notice that this book includes an appendix, which lists some additional synopsis examples that you can use to expand what you've learned so far. I definitely recommend scrolling through to further internalize some of the important points we went over in this book.

I've read a nonfiction book or two in my time, and I know how easy it is to finish a book and say, "that was really helpful," and never apply any of its concepts for the rest of your life. I've definitely been guilty of that before. I think the reason we tend to do this is because it can be overwhelming to try to figure all of this out at once, so we just block any of it from entering into our lives.

Here's what I recommend you do instead. Take one or two points from the book that you'll try to apply right away. Use them in your description writing and whenever you're attempting to market your book. Then, when you have the time and the energy, go through the entire book one more time. Create your synopsis using the exercises at the end of each chapter. Then go through the checklist in Chapters 8 and 9 to fully flesh out the best, most exciting parts of your characters and plot. When you put it all in place, you're bound to get more sales and more attention in the marketplace.

Thank you so much for reading this book. It truly does mean a lot to me and I hope beyond hope that you have the success you crave as an author and a very creative marketer. Go out there and make your synopsis sizzle!

Appendix: Additional Synopsis Examples

The Algorithm by CL Walker

Jon is about to become one of the foremost experts in digital security. Contracted to test the defenses of the largest corporation in history, all he has to do is steal a bit of insignificant data. His success should be the pinnacle of his career. He never expected it to threaten his life.

Shortly after Jon's successful sanctioned hack, a man breaks into his office and mercilessly assaults his coworkers. Someone wants the data Jon stole, and he's willing to kill to get it. When Jon goes on the run, he's chased at every turn. The government, local gangs, foreign spies, and even London's ubiquitous camera network are all turned against him.

As he dashes through the city streets, the computer expert can easily calculate his chances of survival: they're next to impossible.

Burnout by Larry A. Winters

Jessie Black's successful prosecution of a serial murder and rapist put her on the path to stardom at the Philadelphia District Attorney's Office. Public defender Jack Ackerman represented the opposition, and his spectacular public breakdown after the trial put him in a mental institution and gave Frank Ramsey a second chance at freedom.

When Ramsey petitions the court for a new trial with a claim that Ackerman was ineffective, Black must step up to defend him. To keep a convicted killer off the streets, she'll need to prove Ackerman's sanity–a fact she's far from sure of. As she prepares for trial, powerful forces conspire to put Ramsey back on the streets. Black has one chance to keep Ramsey behind bars, and it'll be the toughest fight of her career.

The God Decrees by Mark E. Cooper

Julia is pure dedication. The 19-year-old gymnast works herself to the bone each day to prepare for the upcoming Olympic Games. A competition she'll never reach.

When she's summoned by a wizard to save his people, she'll be stranded on an alien world where women are sheltered, magic is real, and there's no way home. As she comes to terms with her new role, she must make new allies and friends if she wants any chance of survival.

Rune Gate by Mark E. Cooper

Alexandra Yorke was a top police clairvoyant until her lies got the best of her. She isn't a clairvoyant. Alex is a witch, and years of living inside the heads of serial killers has taken its toll. Unable to control her gifts any longer, she retreats from the world.

After a few months of peace at her grandparents' farm, a friend in need asks for help. She reluctantly agrees. When evidence at a murder scene points to witches, Alex becomes the prime suspect. She knew she never should've left grandma's.

Wildest Dreams by Suzi Hixon

Aurelia lives a life without control. The beautiful eldest daughter of a military general, she's had her impending marriage selected for her. She doesn't love Gallus, and she knows she never will. But how can she disobey the wishes of her powerful father?

Resigned to her fate, Aurelia is preparing for her marriage ceremony when she's awoken by a trail of phosphorescent mushrooms. Intrigued, she follows the colorful path into a forest and right into the midst of a druid werebear shifter!

It doesn't take long to realize that the sexy shifter Maol is her one true love. Maol asks if Aurelia wants to join his bear clan, and she jumps at the chance. For the first time in her life, she feels like she's in control of her own destiny. The feeling doesn't last long.

Her father kidnaps Maol's mother and threatens the shifter's life unless Aurelia returns. Aurelia must decide if her freedom and love are worth being disowned by her country, her friends, and her family.

Unknown Threat by Robin Lyons

Cole Judson "Mac" MacKenna is a man in transition. He spent 20 years as a pararescueman in an elite special ops group with the U.S. Air Force. After two decades of action-packed missions, he takes a position at a prestigious public school. Soon enough, his former life of loaded weapons and death-defying rescues has been replaced by arrogant parents, self-serving politicians, and questionable employees.

When unknown assailants start using children for target practice and a well-connected parent abuses one of Mac's students, he'll spring into action like the good old days. Unfortunately for Mac, meddling with the rich can have deadly consequences.

The Galapagos Incident by Felix R. Savage

Evicting people from their homes is a crappy job, but

Elfrida Goto knows that somebody has to do it. If she can't evict the squatters from asteroid 11073 Galapagos, it'll further delay a project she deeply cares about: terraforming Venus. Unfortunately, Elfrida's remote telepresence robot isn't cooperating, and neither are the asteroid's inhabitants. When a terrifying enemy attacks her home base and heads straight for Galapagos, her mission changes in a hurry.

Teaming up with a wannabe Star Force pilot, Elfrida has a plan to save the squatters. If she survives long enough to put it into practice, she'll go up against the most dangerous enemy humanity has ever known…

Wylie Westerhouse: Ghosts on Tour by Nathan Roden

Wylie was this close to being "America's Brand New Voice." When his manager broke the law and fled the country with Wylie's girlfriend, his one chance at success spiraled down the drain. Nowadays, managing a music store pays the bills while Wylie plays the clubs in Branson, Missouri. A new friendship, however, could change everything…

Holly can see ghosts. Ever since her family moved into a Scottish castle, she's been able to communicate with the dead. When a flood kills local tourism and forces Holly and her uncle to sell the castle, she follows the castle's ghostly inhabitants… all the way to Branson.

After Holly accidentally shares her "gift" with Wylie, the magic girl and the musician must team up to save the castle from a group of Branson ghosts out for much more than blood.

Road to Shandara by Ken Lozito

College senior Aaron Jace is ready to start life in the real world. After the unexpected death of his grandfather, Aaron finds an unbelievable note that will change his path for good. The unknowing descendant of an ancient and powerful family, Aaron is thrust into a struggle that began long ago and will reach across worlds to pull him into the fight.

When he learns of the world of Safanar, it seems to be the stuff of legends: dragons, castles, and technologically-advanced cities. But it's as much a dream as it is a nightmare. Danger lurks in the shadows, and a demon sentinel named Tarimus wants to steal Aaron's power before he can learn his full potential. With the help of an imprisoned Safanarion guardian, two mystical swords, and a puzzling family heirloom, Aaron must journey from Earth to find the fabled land of his ancestors. It may be a path that's impossible to survive.

Recycling Humanity by Heather Lee Dyer

As mankind clings to life in space habitats above their dying home, 17-year-old Kaci Lee is hopeful of the future. After all, she worked countless hours to get her space pilot's license, the first of many meticulously-planned lifetime goals. She's well on her way to achieving everything she's ever wanted.

Unforeseen dangers during a routine recycling mission force Kaci to land on the mostly-evacuated Earth. Surprisingly, she meets Abishai on the planet's surface, the handsome son of a famous and mentally-unstable scientist, Dr. Kincaid. Together, Kaci and Abishai must survive in the face of radiation sickness and a freak superstorm. Little do they know that Abishai's father possesses the greatest danger of them all.

Dr. Kincaid has a secret. A secret that could kill Kaci. A secret that could wipe what's left of the human race.

Lord Ruin by Carolyn Jewel

There's a reason Ruan Bettancourt, the Duke of Cynssyr, has obtained the nickname Lord Ruin. His plan in London is to marry the city's most beautiful debutante, and he always gets what he wants.

Spinster Anne Sinclair is sensible, strong, and overlooked. On a night in which she vowed to protect her sister from the infamous Lord Ruin, she never expected to end up in bed with him.

Forced into a marriage neither of them wanted, Anne and the Duke believe they have no hope of passion or love for the rest of their lives. When the rogue falls completely for his tall, bespectacled wife, it's up to him to convince Anne to relinquish her heart.

The Reluctant Debutante by Jean Jacobsen

New York City, 1830. Clarissa Tanner is carefree and joyous until the sudden death of her parents. Forced to pay off family debts, she's given one choice: auction off her beloved horses or reluctantly enter society to face the dreaded marriage market.

Nicholas is a man on a mission. The French artist is hunting for his missing brother who got mixed up with the wrong crowd at the wrong time. To pay his way, Nicholas takes a position as a dance instructor, providing refresher lessons to the beautiful but distracted Clarissa.

As Clarissa trains her thoroughbreds and Nicholas continues his search, the two find a connection through grief and movement. With the auction looming, Clarissa wonders if she could possibly lose her parents and the man of her dreams in rapid succession.

Mistress by Blackmail by Caro LeFever

Darcy Morgan is a poor but determined artist. When she finds out that her best friend is being forced into an arranged marriage, she refuses to stand for the injustice. Darcy marches right into the boardroom of a high-powered company to demand that her friend's brother Marcus end the arrangement.

Marcus La Rocca can see the fire in Darcy's eyes, and he doesn't like it one bit. To keep her as far away from his brother as possible, Marcus blackmails her into being his pretend mistress. After transporting her into a high society life of luxury, Marcus can hardly believe her resistance to his gifts… and his charms.

As Darcy feels her contention begin to slip, and Marcus finds himself falling for her, an unlikely pair draws closer and closer together. After pasts riddled with pain, can Darcy and Marcus let themselves love again?

Kick Up the Dust by Suzi Hixon

Charlie and Sammie are recent high school graduates and the "it" couple of Crowley, Texas. Everybody in town is counting down the days to when the pair will make it permanent, but life has other plans in mind.

When Sammie gets an offer for the start of a professional modeling career in New York, she has no idea why Charlie won't even fight for her to stay. Is he encouraging her to live out her dreams, or does he just want her out of the picture?

Charlie doesn't have time to think about Sammie's new life on the East Coast. A series of droughts has led to a water shortage throughout town, and Charlie's the only one willing to seek out a new water source. Along comes Alina, a former high school nerd turned beautiful and brilliant water witch.

Alina may be Charlie's only chance at saving the town, but will she also be the temptation that finally severs his ties with Sammie for good?

The Rock and the Rainbow Serpent by Vicky McGahey

Feisty Aussie twins Jonathan and Penny Lake come from a long line of powerful wizards. They should've known they'd have to follow in their ancestors' footsteps by saving the world!

The dastardly Blotmorgue family dabbles in the dark arts, much to the dismay of the attendees of the Lakes' School of Wizardry. When a powerful relic, the Hourglass of Lochleigh, is revealed to the world, Baron Blotmorgue seeks control of the Hourglass at all costs. His reckless pursuit of power can only lead to disaster.

Jonathan and Penny must join with Yuri, an Australian Aboriginal, and Seana, a distant English relative, if they want any chance of stopping the Blotmorgues. The young wizards-in- training must combat the evil of the Hourglass or the world as they know it will be consumed by darkness.

Wooly Meets the Chickens by Susanne Blumer

Can a dog and a chicken become best friends?

It's Wooly's first day at Huckleberry Farm, and he can't

wait to make some friends. When he hears the rooster crowing, he knows the chickens are the perfect animals for the job.

Butterscotch, the leader of the chicken coop, isn't so sure. After all, who ever heard of a big dog becoming friends with an entire flock of chickens? He just won't stand for it.

Can Wooly convince Butterscotch to give friendship a try?

About the Author

Bryan Cohen is a fiction and nonfiction author of over 30 books, which have been downloaded a quarter of a million times. With Jim Kukral, he's the co-host of the Sell More Books Show, which discusses the latest self-publishing news each week. Bryan has written over 300 book descriptions for fellow authors, several of which have reached the top 25 in the Amazon store.

He lives with his wife, their cat, and their Netflix account in Chicago.

Acknowledgements

Self-publishing is a misnomer. I couldn't have written this book without help from dozens of people. First and foremost, thank you to the Sizzling Synopsis Launch Team (89 people strong!) for helping me to ensure the book's reception was stellar. My students in my Selling for Authors premium course have taught me so much about teaching copywriting, and this book would've been problematic at best without your "student-teaching." As always, the listeners of The Sell More Books Show were incredibly supportive. Your dedication to the show spurred me on during difficult writing and editing days.

Zizi turned in a wonderful cover, and Ashley Lankford did a great job taking my error-ridden prose and increasing the readability. Sheridan Stancliff helped me to organize all of the description examples, and she made sure the whole ship kept running while I worked on this. Best assistant ever! Other thanks to Honoree Corder, K.M. Weiland, Chris Fox, Simon Whistler, Alida Winternheimer, Robert Scanlon, Dave Chesson, Jim Kukral, and everybody else who helped me spread the word!

Lastly, thanks to Amy. Others may read my books, but you're the one who has to read my mind.

Many thanks!
Sincerely,
Bryan

Thanks From Bryan

Thank you so much for checking out How to Write a Sizzling Synopsis.

It'll make my book sound better for other authors if you leave a review. If you'd be willing to post even just a short sentence or two, I'd really appreciate it.

To learn more about book descriptions, visit www.sellingforauthors.com

Printed in Poland
by Amazon Fulfillment
Poland Sp. z o.o., Wrocław